How To Build A Computer

Build Your Own PC

The Easy Step by Step Guide to Build the Ultimate Custom PC

© Copyright 2006 – BN Publishing

ISBN   9562913252

www.bnpublishing.com

info@bnpublishing.com

Printed in the U.S.A.

How To Build A Computer

Build Your Own PC

Table of Contents

3.   <u>Secondary Components</u>

    1.   Graphics Card

    2.   CD/DVD

    3.   Floppy Drive

    4.   Sound Card

    5.   Modem

4.   <u>Peripherals</u>

    1.   Keyboard & Mouse

    2.   Printer & Scanner

    3.   Monitor

    4.   Speakers

5.   <u>Building the physical computer</u>

            <u>Preparation</u>

            Safety Precautions

10. <u>Software</u>

    1.   Windows

    2.   Linux

11. <u>Optimizing and Overclocking Your New Computer</u>

<u>Overclocking</u>

    1.   Things that can't be overclocked

    2.   Components

    3.   Getting the few extra MHz out of a chip

Choosing the parts

Before you jump onto the web and start spending lots of money on expensive computer parts. You have two questions you should answer that will guide your purchases:

1.   What are you going to use your new computer for?

2.   Will parts be available to use from your old computer?

Choosing the Parts

Decisions, Decisions, Decisions

What am I going to use my new computer for?

Instead of going to the store or an online shop and just buying components, great care must be taken in selecting components. First, decide what you want to use the computer for. The reason you have to consider this is that you may be able to save money by only spending money where it is needed. For instance, for an office computer, you will not need much in the way of graphics power. But you could spend more money on the keyboard, since that is where you will be spending a lot of your time at the computer.

On the other hand, somebody who is going to be playing the latest games on their new computer is going to need a lot more graphics power. However, they may not want to spend much on computer peripherals such as scanners, printers, or webcameras, because they have no interest in such devices. On the other hand, someone may want a computer that offers both office and gaming experiences, and in that case they should expect to spend additional money on peripheral devices, along with high-powered internal components.

Another situation that you should consider when purchasing parts is how well you want the computer to perform. For example, many differing speeds of computer can offer Internet browsing and word-processing capabilities; however, one computer might be faster than another at such tasks. As mentioned above, for an office computer, the main components for speed are the processor, memory (RAM), system bus, and hard drive. If the computer is for gaming, the addition of a high-end graphics accelerator expansion card also becomes a major area which greatly affects computing performance and speed.

Do I plan on overclocking my computer?

If you plan to <u>overclock</u> your components, some parts respond to overclocking better than others. If you are going to seriously overclock your computer, you need to do research into the components you are buying. Components that respond well to heavy overclocking are generally more expensive, although the value of a component is by no means a guarantee of its overclocking potential.

Can I use any of the parts from my old computer?

The answer to this question is unique in nearly every situation. To start, is your old computer available to take spare parts out of? There are usually several reasons why it wouldn't be.

1. You want to sell your old computer.
2. You want to use your old computer for another use, such as using it as a server of some sort.
3. Your old computer is too old, or is completely broken, and so it will be of no use.

In the first situation, you want to sell the old computer. In order to do this, you need enough parts in order for the computer to function correctly. These include: graphics card, hard drive, motherboard, processor, power supply and ram. However, it is usually a kind gesture to leave, at least, a rudimentary sound card and an ethernet card so the person you are selling your computer to can use a network and play sounds. Other than these basic parts, you can use the other parts for your new computer if they meet the other criteria above.

Along with using some parts if you are selling a computer, you can also use non-vital parts if you want to use the old computer as a server. For example, if you plan to reuse your old computer as a utility server, you can easily remove parts such as external drives and the sound card, as these have no use in a server, and they can easily be reused in your new computer, if they are of good enough quality and if they're good enough to withstand new technology.

Another important fact to remember is that sometimes you may not be able to use old parts because they do not work with your new computer. For example, even if you recently upgraded to a very fast AGP card, if your new motherboard has a PCI-Express 16x slot, you will have to get a new graphics card. RAM from your old computer will also often be unusable in your new motherboard.

Since monitor technology moves quite slowly, you can probably take that and use it on the new computer. The same can go for keyboards (unless you want to upgrade your keyboard to a better model), as well as mice, printers, scanners, and possibly speaker sets. On the inside, you may be able to take out the floppy drive, CD-ROM drive, and possibly the sound card and hard drive (depending on how good they are, of course). Sometimes so much is used from the old computer, that the line between an upgrade and new computer is blurred.

Reusing a hard drive from an older computer is an easy way to keep your data from your old computer

Where to find the parts

Once you have decided what you are going to primarily use your computer for, and you have reviewed which parts are available for reuse, you should make a list of what components you will need to actually build your computer. Always research the best components for your computer's application, and be sure on the exact specifications that you will need, as this will save a lot of time and effort when you start shopping around. Make sure that you understand all terminology related to components before you purchase, as this can also save a lot of confusion later in the process.

The internet is usually the best place to start when purchasing parts, and there are many sites that will help you find them. Local PC shops generally also sell components for you to build with, if you can't find suitable vendors online. Trade shows that occur from time to time also provide a good place to shop, as the prices are often significantly reduced.Also, check your local town dump. They may have a special section for computers & monitors that others have gotten rid of. Many times these are more or less brand new computers with such trivial problems as a busted power supply or faulty cables. Of course if the dump does have such a section, it is wise to ask permission of those in charge. They're usually glad to let you go through it, but don't leave a mess. Taking advantage of this can yield incredible finds, with a price tag of free.

OEM vs Retail

Most hardware manufacturers will sell the same components in OEM and Retail versions. Retail hardware is intended to be sold to the end-user through retail channels, and will come fully packaged with manuals, accessories, software, etc. OEM stands for "original equipment manufacturer"; items labeled as such are sold in bulk and are intended for use by firms which may integrate the components into their own products.

However, many online stores will offer OEM hardware at cheaper prices than the corresponding retail versions. You will usually receive such an item by itself in an anti-static bag. It may or may not come with a manual or a CD containing drivers. Warranties on OEM parts may often be shorter, and sometimes require you to obtain support through your vendor, rather than the manufacturer. Other than that, OEM components themselves are usually the same as their retail counterparts.

What should affect the choice of any part/peripherial?

This section lists things that should be taken account of with every single choice when selecting parts. Considering some parts these things are more obvious than with others.

Compatibility

Do your parts and peripherials work together? Do they work with the software of your choice? Choosing parts that work with any other operating system than the most mainstream one is often a guarantee that they work with many other operating systems too than just those two. This is good because you can change your mind later. So even if you're building a computer to run Windows, choosing hardware that would run a Linux system might be a good thing.

Ergonomy

Ergonomy is most important when choosing peripherials such as keyboard or a mouse, but also the ease of assembly is important when choosing parts.

Noise

This is important especially if you're going to sleep in the same room with your computer and have it turned on. It may be useful to have a computer on 24/7 because computers are usually slow to start up and shutdown. If you're turning your computer on and off before and after each use, something like checking your e-mail takes a lot more time. Note that a computer is only as quiet as its noisiest part (or peripheral).

So where does computer noise come from? Some components, like hard disk drives and CD drives, produce noise, especially the higher speed drives. Usually, the loudest noise comes from a computer's cooling fan or fans. Smaller fans produce more noise for the amount of work they do.

Operating temperature

The computer has to be cooled down so it doesn't break. Parts with high operating temperatures need more cooling and noiseless cooling is hard to find as well as being far more expensive than their noisy counterparts. Parts and peripherials with high operating temperatures also tend to warm up the room when the system is cooled by air, so the room may need cooling too. Manufacturers assume the computer will be kept in a room that has an air conditioner kept roughly at "room temperature" (apx 73F or 22C) but, typically parts are expected to be able to handle more extreme conditions. More heat can tend to decrease stability and increase the elements that break down components slowly over time, so better cooling increases the stability as well as lifetime of your system.

Price

There are always new hype features in stores. Many of them are good, but buying hardware one model older may result in better price/quality-relation, when the new features aren't exactly needed.

Power

The speed of a processor, the size of memory, resolution of monitor, printer or a scanner. Find out what is enough and look for the best price/quality-relation matching your need and budget.

Core Components

These are the components that will be the core of your new computer. It is impossible to put together a computer without these components and a bare set of peripherals.

Chassis (Case) & Power Supply

This was probably the most overlooked part of the whole computer at one stage. Most cases were beige, and since most components drew far less power than similar components do now, power supplies were never talked about. Recently, however, cases have become considerably more attractive, and people spend a sizable amount of their upgrade budgets on lights and glow-in-the-dark cables. Cases now come in millions of styles, and colours to suit anyone's taste.

People are spending more money on cases now than they ever have before. If you are only building an office computer, the style of case will be of little concern to you, so you might only want a inexpensive ATX case (ATX is the specification which makes them the same size, so you can put the same parts inside), and an inexpensive power supply, since you won't be running high-end processors or high-end graphic cards. Keep in mind not to buy a power supply with a sleeve bearing fan, as these are of considerably less quality. As a guide, you will not want a power supply with a rating of less than 300 watts, as you may likely not be able to power all the parts in your computer with a power supply with a lower rating. Most case-power supply bundles are adequate, but tend to be of a lower quality than power supplies that are sold separately from cases.

For cases and power supply there are 5 things to consider.

- **Formfactor**: For general use, the ATX formfactor is recomended because it allows your computer to be easily expanded, and is the most common standart formfactor for computers. Micro ATX is smaller than vanilla ATX, but at the cost of fewer expansion slots. Flex ATX is even smaller than Micro ATX, but only allows 2 expansion slots. BTX is another formfactor designed for more efficiant cooling that has not cought on yet. Many OEM computers use non-standard formfactors.

- 'Number of storage Drive Space'. Internal Hard Drives/Floppy Drives (go in the so called small bays) and Internal DVD Drives (go in the large bays) take up space in the case.. so make sure you consider how many you have.. usually its a good idea to calculate using the motherboard.

```
Number of IDE x2
Number of FDD x2
Number of SATA
Number of SCSI2 (estimated)

eg. for a motherboard with one FDD, one IDE, 4 SATA
no SCSI..
its best to choose one with at least 8 slots...

4 BIG + 4 SMALL = for 4 optical + 3 hard drives + 1
floppy
```

This is the mid-tower configuration. For smaller computers with less storage drives.. like 1 Hard Drive, 2 Optical Drives get a mini-tower (2 BIG + 2 SMALL) cause it saves space

- 'Power Rating': A too small power number doesn't run your high power devices (like optical, CPU and Graphics Cards). For certain graphics cards (especially high end ones with inbuilt fans), a recommendation of 350W is required. In general, if your motherboard has a 24 pin power connector, choose one which is at least 300W as the 4 extra pins are for high power applications. When in doubt, buy a more powerful PSU.

- Case FAN: yes... some cases have case fans... and make sure you choose one which matches your CPU interface on the motherboard. Although most motherboards fit most cases... its the position of the case fan that affects speed and stability of the system as a good case have the fan aiming directly at the CPU fan for good cooling effects.

If you plan on building a high end gaming PC, you might want a case that looks good, and a much more potent power supply. For the more aesthetically inclined, there are countless companies who make designer cases that will suit many personal preferences. A power supply with more than 400 watts is usually more than is required by most people, and will allow you to power high-end graphics cards, cooling systems, and aesthetic enhancements such as cold cathode lights, cooling equipment, and other such things.

In all cases you should try to check reviews from a computer hardware site before you decide to purchase a power supply; quality can vary greatly and wattage output is frequently overstated. Quality power is also usually more efficient, so it will produce less heat and its fans can run at lower, quieter speeds. Manufacturers sometimes try to make passive, or fanless, power supplies, but in most cases they will end up running dangerously hot, and so are only suitable if you plan to add your own cooling solution.

CPU (Processor)

The Central Processing Unit (CPU) is the heart of your computer as it performs nearly all functions that requires extensive processing power. Therefore, it is very important that you choose a suitable CPU for your function as the choice of CPU directly affects the speed and stability of your system.

Before we can explain differences between CPUs, you must first be familiar with certain CPU properties.

Clock Speed, measured in Gigahertz (GHz), or Megahertz (MHz) on older systems is the number of calculation cycles that your CPU can perform per second. Therefore, a higher clock speed generally points toward a faster system. But not all CPUs perform an equal quantity of work per cycle, meaning two CPUs at the same clock speed can potentially perform at very different levels.

Front Side Bus Speed (FSB) is the rate at which the CPU communicates with the motherboard Front Side Bus components in MHz. A larger FSB value shows that your CPU is able to communicate with other components on the motherboard (and thus your system) faster.

Interface: CPUs must be connect to motherboards via a series of connectors. It is VERY important that your CPU interface is a COMPLETE MATCH to your motherboard CPU socket otherwise you would be wasting money on a piece of spare silicon.

Bit-Rate: Most modern CPUs are of the 32-bit system which work fine with most modern operating system and hardware. Higher end models are the 64-bit system which may allow faster CPU processing capabilities due to the larger band-width, but not all operating systems are compatible with the newer 64-bit format.

Hyper Threading (HT): Hyper-threading is a new technology of parallel processing which instead of one single core, your CPU is able to have separate cores working on different tasks which greatly speeds up the system speed. However, Hyper Threading technology requires a motherboard that supports Hyperthreading technology and are generally very expensive.

Manufacture and Model: There are two main manufactures of CPUs Intel and AMD, each having advantages and disadvantages that would be explained below.

L2-Cache: the amount of Memory dedicated for the CPU in MB, generally, the larger the L2 cache, the faster your system would run.

Now, one of the most common mistakes of choosing a CPU is by ignoring the fine print of CPU specifications while relying completely on the clock speed. CPUs specs are written in full, I give a brief explanation of the spec, eg.

```
Intel Pentium 4 3.2GHz LGA775 FSB800 HT L2-2MB

Model: Intel Pentium 4
Clock Speed: 3.2GHz (=3200MHz)
```

```
Interface: Land Grid Array 775
L2-Cache: 1MB (=1024 kB)
Other Spec: HT technology
```

The consumer logic for processor speed may be misleading because many consumers think that clock speed, which is measured in gigahertz (GHz) or megahertz (MHz) is equal to system speed. While the higher the clock speed the CPU is able to do cycles more frequently and it does have a fundamental effect on speed, it is not the sole factor as the number of calculations per cycle is different for each different manufacturer and model.

Intel classifies its CPUs using a series of numbers. 3xx, 4xx, 5xx, 6xx and 7xx of which 7xx being the highest end products. Generally, the higher the number, the faster the CPU and the more expensive. usually, models and ratings correspond.

- 3xx Series: Intel Celeron (L2-128KB)

- 4xx Series: Intel Celeron D (L2-512KB)

- 5xx Series: Intel Pentium 4 / Celeron D (L2-1MB)

- 6xx Series: Intel Pentium 4 / Pentium 4 XE (L2-2MB)

- 7xx Series: Intel Pentium 4 XE

the number followed by suffix J signifies XD technology

eg.

```
Intel  Pentium  4  3.0GHz  L2-1MB  with  HT  -->  Intel
Pentium 4 530J
```

AMD CPUs are even more confusing in classification. The AMD Athlon CPU rating are NOT of the actual clock speed but rather the equivalence bench mark performance corresponding to a

Pentium 4 CPU. The conversion Table is as follows,

```
AMD Athlon 1500+ = Actually runs at 1.33 GHz
AMD Athlon 1600+ = Actually runs at 1.40 GHz
AMD Athlon 1700+ = Actually runs at 1.47 GHz
AMD Athlon 1800+ = Actually runs at 1.53 GHz
AMD Athlon 1900+ = Actually runs at 1.60 GHz
AMD Athlon 2000+ = Actually runs at 1.67 GHz
AMD Athlon 2100+ = Actually runs at 1.73 GHz
AMD Athlon 2200+ = Actually runs at 1.80 GHz
AMD Athlon 2400+ = Actually runs at 1.93 GHz
AMD Athlon 2500+ = Actually runs at 1.833 GHz
AMD Athlon 2600+ = Actually runs at 2.133 GHz
AMD Athlon 2700+ = Actually runs at 2.17 GHz
AMD Athlon 2800+ = Actually runs at 2.083 GHz
AMD Athlon 3000+ = Actually runs at 2.167 GHz
AMD Athlon 3200+ = Actually runs at 2.20 GHz
```

In choosing different manufacturers and models, the CPU would generally be dictated by the way your intend to use your computer. AMD CPUs are generally less expensive than Intel CPUs of the same clock speed but there are great differences in the CPU architechture. Intel Pentium 4 is specifically designed to optimise clock speed while the number of calculations per cycle is reduced. Therefore, benchmark tests of the speed of the AMD Athlon XP 3000+ is approximately the same as Intel Pentium 4 3.2GHz. Most gamers prefer AMD CPUs because of cheaper price for a faster speed, however, graphic designers and professionals prefer Intel CPUs due to their Hyper Threading technology.

You may wish to purchase a high end AMD64/emt64 processor, which provides support for 64-bit operating system (eg. Windows XP Professional 64-bit Edition). A 64-bit system is very efficient in handling large amounts of RAM. A 32-bit system efficiency drops beyond about 512 to 864MB of RAM, and becomes significantly less efficient beyond 4GB of RAM.

A 64-bit processor is currently an expensive investment as most applications run on the 32-bit system. However, there is no doubt that the 32-bit system would gradually be replaced by the 64-bit system when the prices fall over a few years time. It is unlikely that the 64-bit system would completely replace the 32-bit system within 5 years but Linux users might find a great improvement in speed when a 64-bit processor is used.

Smaller processors are generally preferred for overclocking, as they run cooler, and can achieve higher clock speeds. Retail CPU's come in a package containing a HSF (Heat Sink Fan), instructions, and a warranty, often 3 years. OEM CPUs do not include these.

The current CPU speeds and advantages change frequently, so for up-to-date comparisons, you may want to check a website that specialises in Hardware reviews, such as Tom's Hardware Guide or Anandtech

CPU Cooling

CPU cooling is very important and should not be overlooked. A less than average CPU temperature prolongs CPU life (to more than 10 years). On the other hand high CPU temperatures can cause unreliable operation, such as computer freezes, or slow operation. Extremely high temperatures can cause immediate CPU destruction by melting the materials in the chip and changing the physical shape of the sensitive transistors on the CPU. Because of this, **never** switch on the computer if your CPU has no cooling at all. It is an extremely stupid thing to do, the scenario of 'I'll just test whether my CPU works!' as by doing so, you would find that the CPU frys in less than 5 seconds and you will be off to buy a new one.

Most CPU installations use forced-air cooling, but convection cooling and water cooling are also options. For traditional forced-air cooling, the heat sink and fan (HSF) included in most retail CPUs is usually sufficient to cool the CPU at stock speed. Overclockers might want to use a more powerful aftermarket fan, or even try water cooling because they need additional cooling ability given the increased heat of overclocking.

HSFs with decent performance are usually copper-based. The cooling effect is enhanced if the HSF has heatpipes. Silent (i.e. Fanless) HSFs are there to provide users a nearly silent cooling.

Many retail heatsink+fan units have a thermal pad installed, which transfers heat from the CPU to the fan helping diffuse the heat created by the CPU. This pad is usable only once. If you wish to remove the fan from another CPU so that you can use it on your new one, or need to take it off for some reason, you will need to remove it, and apply a thermal paste or another thermal pad. Note that some of the cheaper pads can melt in unexpected heat and may cause problems and potentially even damage if you are overclocking. In either case, thermal paste is usually more effective, just harder to apply. If you plan to do any high performance computing, or removing and replacing the HSF, often thermal paste is suggested. If you are planning a long term installation a thermal pad is suggested. Non-conductive thermal pastes made up of silicon are the cheapest and safest.

Silver-based thermal pastes sometimes perform better than normal thermal pastes, and carbon-based ones perform better still. When applied improperly both can be conductive, causing electrical shorts upon contact with the motherboard. A thin properly-applied layer will usually prevent this problem, though some pastes can become runny when they get hot. Users should also beware that many "silver" thermal pastes do not actually contain any silver metal.

For quiet operation, start with a low-heat (low number of watts) CPU. Processors made by VIA, such as the VIA C3, tend to produce low amounts of heat. The Pentium M gives performance that is on par with many of the desktop processors, but gives off more heat than the Via processors. You can also underclock your

CPU, giving up some unneeded performance for some peace and quiet. Another option is to choose a large copper heat sink with an open fin pattern. However, true fanless operation is difficult to achieve in most case designs. You can position a case fan to blow across the heat sink, or mount a fan on the heat sink. With either choice of fan placement, choose a large and slow fan over a small and fast fan to decrease noise and increase air flow.

Motherboard

I cannot stress more that the motherboard is the MOST important part of your computer. It is worth investment in a decent motherboard rather than a CPU (although if financially acceptable, both) as your motherboard is what connects different parts of the computer together. A good motherboard allows a modest CPU and RAM to run at max efficiently whereas a bad motherboard allows high end products to run only modestly.

There are 6 things one must consider in choosing a motherboard, CPU Interface, Chipset, IDE or SATA support, Expansion Slot Interfaces and Other Connectors

'CPU Interface' The CPU interface Must be an EXACT MATCH to your CPU spec as a LGA775 CPU would not fit a socket 478 motherboard and basically you've wasted money on a spare piece of silicon. Intel currently has two mainstream formats, the older Socket 478 (which is gradually being phased out) and the newer

Land Grid Array 775, which supports higher end CPU with HT technology due to its more efficeint transfer rate. AMD currently uses two sockets, 754 and 939. Socket 754 is being aimed at the value market, with all new performance CPUs being released for Socket 939.

Formfactor You must choose a motherboard that can fit inside of your case.

'Chipset' Chipsets are also important as it determines the efficiency of RAM and Expansion slots Intel 915 supports upto 533MHz DDRII RAM Intel 925 supports upto 600MHz DDRII RAM

The functions of BIOS is highly important. Some BIOS features crash proof functions essentail for updating the firmware. Other motherboards allow BIOS control of overclocking of CPU, RAM and Graphics card which are much stable and safer for overclocking.

'IDE (ATA) or SATA interface' Older PCs have the two IDE interface which are parallel 44 pin connectors but as the motherboard cannot access two devices connected on the same IDE port simultaneously, this has caused a draw back in speed of hard drives and DVD-drives. The newer serial ATA (SATA) interface has 4 separate slots that allow independent access and thus increases the speed of which hard drives and DVD drives work.

'Expansion Slot Interfaces' Old motherboards have the following slots:

- AGP - for graphics cards (ranging from AGP 1x, 2x, 4x and 8x)
- PCI - for expansion cards and obsolete low end graphics cards

Due to the evolution of new graphics cards on the serial PCI-Express Technology, current newer motherboards have the following connections:

- PCI-Express 16x - for mainstream graphics cards (4 times speed of AGP 8x)
- PCI-Express 1x - for faster expansion cards (replacing older PCI)
- PCI - for use of old expansion cards (would be phased out)

Older AGP 8x graphics cards are generally being phased out for PCI-Express 16x as the speed and efficiency mounts to about 4 times efficient of the PCI-Express 16x technology... Old PCI cards are either now on-board the motherboard (for sound cards, LAN cards, IEEE 1394 firewire and USB 2.0 interfaces) or now becoming PCI-Express variants.

'Other Connectors' Some considerations for other connectors and expansions include

- USB - the number and version of USB connectors (USB 1.0, 1.1 or 2.0)
- On-Board Sound Card - Stereo, 3.1, 5.1, 6.1, 7.1, 8.1
- On-Board Graphics Card (Phasing Out)
- On-Board Base 100 LAN Card
- Serial COM or Parallel Printer Ports
- On-Board IEEE 1394 Firewire

I would suggest at least 4 USB 2.0 ports for high speed access. On-Board Graphics cards are generally becoming obsolete as they cannot match the newer PCI-Express 16x technology, especially for gaming where high cooling and efficiency is required.

Most motherboards also come with onboard sound. Onboard sound is more than enough for most users, although if you are particular about audio quality or plan to use your computer to record high-end audio, you may prefer to use a dedicated sound card (preferably PCI-Express 1x). Some high-end motherboards support on-board 5.1 Channel Dolby surround sounds so this may also be a consideration.

If you want gigabit Ethernet, you should purchase a motherboard with the feature built in. By being built into the motherboard, it will have a faster link to all your components than it would through a PCI expansion card. Also, if you'd like to import Digital

Video (DV) onto your system, many motherboards offer onboard FireWire ports.

If you are upgrading an older computer, keep in mind the motherboard's number and type of expansion board slots.

RAM (Random Access Memory)

The amount of RAM you use is dependent on the purpose that you want to use it for. Earlier versions of Windows and Linux will run comfortably, though slowly at times, on 128 MB. Some newer operating systems such as Windows XP require 256MB of RAM to run comfortably. Many people now have 512 MB or more for better performance. Users of modern games and graphics software, or people who may wish to host Internet services such as a Web site, may want 1 GB or more.

Another thing to consider when choosing the amount of RAM for your system is your graphics card. Most motherboard-integrated graphics chips and PCI Express graphics cards marketed with the "Turbo Cache" feature will use system memory to store information related to rendering graphics; this system memory is generally not available at all to the operating system. On average, these graphics processors will use between 16MB and 128MB of system memory for rendering purposes.

The actual type of RAM you will need will depend on the motherboard and chipset you get. Most current motherboards use

DDR (Double Data Rate) RAM. The Intel 915/925 chipsets use DDR2 RAM. Chipsets that use dual-channel memory require you to use two identical (in terms of size and speed) sticks of RAM. Your RAM should usually operate at the same clock speed as the CPU's Front Side Bus (FSB). Your motherboard may not be able to run RAM slower than the FSB, and using RAM faster than the FSB will simply have it run at the same speed as your FSB. Buying low-latency RAM will help with overclocking your FSB, which can be of use to people who want to get more speed from their system.

If you are upgrading from an existing computer, it is best to check with a user group to see if your machine requires specific kinds of RAM. Many computer OEMs, such as Gateway and HP, require custom RAM, and generic RAM available from most computer stores may cause compatibility problems in such systems.

RAM have different bandwidths, ie 400, 533, 600, 733, 800, the current trend is moving from DDR2-400 RAM to DDR2-533 RAM as it is more efficient. Higher end models are very expensive unless you find it worth the investment.

Labeling of RAM

RAM are labelled by its Memory Size (In MB) and clockspeed (or bandwidth).

- SDRAM (Synchronous Dynamic RAM) is labeled by its clock speed in megahertz (MHz). For example, PC133 RAM runs at 133MHz. SDRAM is nearly obsolete as nearly all motherboards have withdrew support for SDRAM. It is now superceded by the more efficient DDR RAM.

128MB SD-133 = 128MB PC133 RAM

- DDR RAM can be labeled in two different ways. It can be labeled by approximate bandwidth; as an example, 400MHz-effective DDR RAM has approximately 3.2GB/s of bandwidth, so it is commonly labeled as PC3200. It can also be labeled by its effective clock speed; 400MHz effective DDR RAM is also known as DDR-400. There is also DDR and DDR2 labelled as PC and PC2.

256MB DDR-400 = 256MB PC2 3200 RAM 256MB DDR2-400 = 256MB PC 3200 RAM

DDR RAM has two versions DDR (also DDRI) and DDR2 (or DDRII)

- DDR supports DDR-100, DDR-200, DDR-300, DDR-400 (mainstrem) and DDR-533 (rare)
- DDR2 supports DDR-400, DDR-533 (mainstrem) and rare/expensive DDR-600, DDR-733, DDR-800, DDR-933, DDR-1066

Hard Drive

Currently when choosing a hard drive, you have a choice between two competing technologies - IDE/Parallel ATA and Serial ATA, the latter being a much newer technology - and an older technology, the Small Computer System Interface, or SCSI (pronounced "scuzzy"). IDE cables can be distinguished by their wide 40-pin connector, coloured first-pin wire, and usually white "ribbon" style cables. This technology is rapidly deteriorating, as it cannot keep up with the increasing speed of current hard drives. IDE based hard drives do not exceed 7,200 RPM, whereas SATA drives reach up to 10,000 RPM.

If you want Serial ATA, you will either need to purchase a motherboard that supports it, or purchase a PCI card that will allow you to connect your hard drive. Few consumer desktop motherboards built today support SCSI, and for building a new computer, the work needed to implement it may be outweighed by the relative simplicity and performance of IDE and SATA.

As a rule-of-thumb minimum, you will need a hard drive capable of holding at least 20GB, although the largest drives available on the market can contain 400GB. Few people will need disks this large - for most people, somewhere in the range of 80-200GB will be sufficient. The amount of space you will need can depend on many factors, such as how many high-end games and programs you want to install, how many media files you wish to store, or how many high-quality videos you want to render. It is usually better to get a hard drive with a capacity slightly larger than you anticipate using, in case you need more in the future. However, should you run out of space, you may add an additional hard drive if you have any free IDE or Serial ATA connectors, or through an external interface, such as USB or FireWire.

One additional consideration when purchasing a hard drive should be the drive warranty. Many manufactures offer warranties ranging from 30 days (typically OEM) up to five years. It is well worth spending an extra few dollars to extend the drive warranty as long as possible.

Secondary Components

These components are important to your computer, but are not as central and necessary as the Core Components.

Graphics Card

Currently, two companies dominate the graphics processing unit, or GPU, field: nVIDIA and ATI. nVIDIA and ATI build their own graphics products, and license their technologies to other companies. Each brand's similar models have comparable performance levels, and each brand has its own supporters. Video cards have their own RAM, and many of the same rules that dominate the motherboard RAM field apply here: the more RAM, and the faster it is, the better the performance will be. Most applications require at least 32MB of video RAM, although 128MB is rapidly becoming the new standard. On the other end, 512MB video cards top the consumer end of the video card market. As a rule of thumb, if you want a high end video card, you need a minimum of 128MB of video memory -- preferably 256MB. Don't be fooled though, memory is only part of the card and the actual video processor is more important than the memory.

It is generally better for you to choose your video card based on your own research, as everyone has slightly different needs. Many video card and chip makers are known to measure their products' performance in ways that you may not find practical. A good video card is often much more than a robust 3D renderer; be sure to examine what you want and need your card to do, such as digital (DVI) output, TV output, multiple-monitor support, built-in TV tuners and video input. Another reason you need to carefully research is that manufacturers will often use confusing model numbers designed to make a card sound better than it is to sell it better. For example, the Geforce 4 MX series of cards claim to be a "Geforce 4," however, the actual processor is closer to a Geforce 2, only more powerful, meaning that these cards actually lack many features available even to the Geforce 3 series. However, when these cards were first produced, they were considerably cheaper than a real Geforce 4 (the TI series) making them an ideal choice if you were more interested in working on a spreadsheet than in playing games. For this sort of reason, you have to carefully pick your card depending on your needs.

Interface There are 3 different Graphics card interfaces, PCI, AGP and PCI-Express

Old video cards use the standard PCI 1x slots that are now obsolete due to limited speed and memory. PCI cannot transfer data very quickly, so a system with such a card will often seem to "jump" or halt for short periods when data is being transfered. These cards are needed for a few rare systems lacking an AGP slot (usually low end desktop systems designed to be cheap.)

Most video cards bought in the last 2 years are of the AGP

standard. There are 4 different speed and bandwidths of AGP, 1x, 2x, 4x and 8x. While 8x is the fastest and most common for high end products. The true performance of your AGP card is limited by the lower AGP value of your graphics card and motherboard. eg. a AGP 8x card on a 4x motherboard can only run on max 4x support. AGP will be phased out and there will not be an AGP 16x due to technical limitations.

The newest trend in grahics card is the PCI-Express system that supports upto 16x speeds. This is new technology and is generally more expensive but it runs at higher speeds. Only newer models such as ATI Radeon X700 or Nvidia GeForce 6800 can run on PCI-Express 16x system. Note that your motherboard must also have the PCI-Express 16x graphics card slot. (Most motherboards have one PCI-E 16x while plenty of PCI-E 1x slots... so make sure you use the right one)

CD/DVD

Optical drives have progressed a long way in the past few years, and you can now easily purchase DVD writers that are capable of burning 9GB of data to a disk for an insignificant amount of money. Even if you don't plan on watching or copying DVDs on your computer, it is still worth purchasing a burner for their superior backup capabilities.

When purchasing a DVD writer, you will want one that is capable of burning both the '+' and '-' standards, and they should also be

Dual Layer compatible. This will ensure that you can burn to almost all recordable DVDs currently on the market (the other major format, DVD-RAM is almost unused, for the most part, so don't worry about it).

Floppy Drive

Though generally not needed, floppy drives are often installed anyway. Floppy drives have been made obsolete in recent years by devices such as USB "Thumb Drives" and CD writers. Floppy drives are sometimes required for BIOS updates and exchanging small files with older computers. Floppy drives block air movement with wide cables, and can make computers set to check the drive take longer to start (most have an option in their bios to disable this.) The drives and disks are also notoriously unreliable. One option to overcome the cable problem and to make it easier to install is to buy an external USB floppy drive. These are potentially a little bit faster and can be plugged into a different system (such as a laptop without a floppy drive.) However, not all systems support booting from a USB floppy drive -- most notably older motherboards. Most newer systems do now though. A USB floppy drive is considerably more expensive and since floppy drives are not needed much anymore, this is rarely a useful option. You can easily get a thumb drive holding > 50x as much as one floppy disk for the same price as a USB drive.

Sound Card

Most motherboards have built-in sound features. These are often adequate for most users. However, you can purchase a good sound card and speakers at relatively low cost - a few dollars at the low end can make an enormous difference in the range and clarity of sound. Also, these onboard systems tend to use more system resources, so you are better off with a real soundcard for gaming.

Good quality in sound cards depends on a few factors. The digital-analog conversion (DAC) is generally the most important stage for general clarity, but it is a poorly measurable process. Reviews, especially those from audiophile sources, are worth consulting for this; but don't go purely by specifications, as many different models with similar specs can produce completely different results. Cards may offer digital (S/PDIF) output, in which case the DAC process is moved from your sound card either to a dedicated receiver or to one built into your speakers.

Sound cards made for gaming or professional music tend to do outstandingly well for their particular purpose. In games various effects are oftentimes applied to the sound in real-time, and a gaming sound card will be able to do this processing on-board, instead of using your CPU for the task. Professional music cards tend to be built both for maximum sound quality and low latency (transmission delay) input and output, and include more and/or different kinds of inputs than those of consumer cards.

Modem

A modem is needed in order to connect to a dial up internet connection. A modem can also be used for faxing. Modems can attach to the computer in different ways, and can have built-in processing or use the computer's CPU for processing.

Modems with built-in processing generally include all modems that connect via a standard serial port, as well as any modems that refer to themselves as "Hardware Modems". Software Modems, or modems that rely on the CPU generally include both Internal and USB modems, or have packaging that mentions drivers or requiring a specific CPU to work.

Modems that rely on the CPU are often designed specifically for the current version of Windows only, and will require drivers that are incompatible with future Windows versions, and may be difficult to upgrade. Software Modems are also very difficult to find drivers for non-Windows operating systems. The manufacturer is unlikely to support the hardware with new drivers after it is discontinued, forcing you to buy new hardware. Most such modems are internal or external USB, but this is not always the case.

Modems can be attached via USB, a traditional serial port, or an internal card slot. Internal and USB modems are more easily autodetected by the operating system and less likely to have problems with setup. USB and serial port modems often require an extra power supply block.

Gaming modems are normal modems that default to having a low compression setting to reduce lag, but are generally no longer used by gamers, who prefer broadband connections.

Ethernet Card

An ethernet card is required in order to connect to a local area network or a cable or DSL modem. These typically come in speeds of 10mbps, 100mbps, or 1000mbps (gigabit); these are designated as 10Mbps, 10/100Mbps, or 10/100/1000Mbps products. The 10/100 and 10/100/1000 parts are most commonly in use today. In many cases, ethernet will be built into a motherboard. Otherwise, you will have to purchase one - these typically are inserted into a PCI slot. For 10/100/1000Mbps ethernet, it is recomended that you use one built into your motherboards chipset.

Peripherals

Your computer and you interact through the peripherals. The keyboard and monitor are pretty much the barest minimum you can go with and still be able to interact with your computer. Your choice in peripherals very much depends on personal preference and the complexity of the interactions you intend to have with your computer.

Keyboard & Mouse

When choosing a mouse, there is generally no reason to not choose an optical mouse. They are considerably lighter (and as such, reduce <u>RSI</u>) as they have no moving parts, they are much better at smoothly tracking movement, and they don't require constant cleaning like ball mice (though it may be wise to brush off the lens with a q-tip or other soft tool on occasion.) Make sure that you spend money on a decent-quality mouse made by companies such as Microsoft or Logitech, as lower-end optical mice will skip if moved too fast. Mice of medium-to-high quality will track the movement almost flawlessly.

Although three buttons are generally enough for operating a computer in normal circumstances, extra buttons can come in handy, as you can add set actions to extra buttons, and they can come in handy for playing First Person Shooter games. One thing to note is that with some mice those extra buttons are not actually seen by the computer itself as extra buttons and will not work properly in games. These buttons use software provided by the manufacturer to function. However, it is sometimes possible to configure the software to map the button to act like a certain keyboard key so that it will be possible to use it in games in this manner.

Wireless keyboards and mice do not have a hugely noticeable delay like they once did, and now also have considerably improved battery life. However, gamers may still want to avoid wireless input devices because the very slight delay may impact gaming activities -- though some of the higher end models have less troubles with this -- and the extra weight of the batteries can be an inconvenience.

Printer & Scanner

For most purposes, a mid-range Inkjet Printer will be more than enough for most people, and you will generally want one that is capable of printing around 4800dpi, and you will also want it to be able to print out fairly quickly. When choosing a printer, always check how much new cartridges cost, as replacement cartridges can often outweigh the actual printer's cost in less than a year. Of course, double check extra information about the printer you are interested in (for example, Epson has protection measures that make refilling your own ink cartridges more difficult because the printer will not see the cartridge as full once it is used up).

For office users that plan to do quite a bit of black and white printing buying a black and white laser printer is now an affordable option, and the savings and speed can quickly add up for home office users printing more than 500 pages a month.

Scanners are useful, especially in office settings, they can function with your printer as a photocopier, and with software can also interact with your modem to send Faxes. When purchasing a

Scanner, check to see how "accessible" it is (does it have one-touch buttons), and check how good the scanning quality is, before you leave the store if possible.

Finally, "Multi-Function Centres" are often a cost-effective solution to purchasing both, as they take up only one port on your computer, and one power point, but remember that they can be a liability, since if one component breaks down, both will need to be replaced.

Display

When choosing a display for your computer, you have two key choices of technology: the Cathode Ray Tube (CRT) screen, or an LCD screen. Both technologies have their advantages and disadvantages: CRTs are generally preferred by gamers and graphic artists, for both the price at which they can be bought and their generally superior response times, but this is offset by the added size and weight that a large screen requires. LCDs are generally more expensive than CRTs, but high-end models are generally preferred for tasks which need higher definition, such as movie editing, and are also popular amongst people with little-to-no desk space, as they do not need as much space as a similarly-sized CRT.

LCD Panels

Liquid Crystal Displays (LCD's) have the advantage of being a completely digital setup, when used with the DVI-D digital connector. When running at the screen's native resolution, this can result in the most stable and sharp image available on current monitors. Many LCD panel displays are sold with an analog 15-pin VGA connector or, rarely, with an analog DVI-I connector. Such displays will be a bit fuzzy, and are generally best avoided for a similarly-sized CRT. If you want an LCD displays, be sure to choose a digital setup if you can; however, manufacturers have chosen to use this feature for price differentiation. The prime disadvantage of LCDs is "dead pixels", which are small failing areas on your monitor, which can be very annoying, but generally aren't covered under warranty - this can make purchasing LCD displays a financial risk. LCDs are generally OK for fast-paced gaming, but you should be sure that your screen has a fairly fast response time (of 25 ms or lower) if you want to play fast games. Nearly all flat panels sold today meet this requirement, some by a factor of 3. When picking an LCD, keep in mind that they are designed to display at one resolution only, so, to reap the benefits of your screen, your graphics card must be capable of displaying at that resolution. That in mind, they can display lower resolutions with a black frame around the outside (which means your entire screen isn't filled), or by stretching the image (which leads to much lower quality). Running at a higher resolution than your monitor can handle will either make everything on the screen smaller, at a significant quality drop, or will display only a part of the screen at a time (which can be annoying).

Cathode Ray Tube Displays

The other key type of display is the CRT or Cathode Ray Tube display. While CRT technology is older it often outperforms LCD technology in terms of response times, color reproduction, and brightness levels, although LCD displays are quickly catching up. There are two types of CRT displays, *shadow mask* and *aperture grill*. An aperture grill display is brighter and perfectly flat in the vertical direction, but is more fragile and has one or two mostly-unnoticeable thin black lines (support wires) running across the screen. CRTs are generally 2-4 times as deep as similarly-sized LCDs, and can weigh around 10 times as much, but this normally isn't a concern unless you will be moving your computer a lot. If you purchase a CRT display over the internet, shipping costs for a CRT can be higher than for an LCD. Since CRTs constantly refresh, the time in which they can refresh is much quicker, which is good for gaming, however, can cause headaches in some people at lower rates, so it may be ideal to pick a screen offering higher update frequencies at whichever resolutions you intend to use. Most people who have problems with low frequencies (60Hz) find it preferable to have at least 80Hz at the intended resolution.

Some won't be bothered by this at all however.

Note that sometimes the CRTs with a flat screen instead of curved are called "flat screens" so this is not to be confused with the term "flat panel" used to refer to LCDs.

Speakers

Computer speaker sets come in two general varieties; 2/2.1 sets (over a wide range of quality), and "surround", "theater", or "gaming" with four or more speakers, which tend to be significantly more expensive. Low-end speakers usually suffer from low bass response or having no amplification, both of which make a huge difference in sound. Powered speakers with separate sub-woofers usually cost only a few dollars more and make a significant difference. At the higher end, one should start to see features like standard audio cables (instead of manufacturer-specific ones), built in DACs, and a separate control box. The surround sets are usually identical to the 2.1 set of a manufacturer, just with more speakers, which can be useful for gaming or movie watching. 5.1 and 7.1 support are becoming standard now, however, it is still necessary that you ensure your sound hardware is capable of 5.1/7.1 before buying a speaker system for this. If you have a lot of money you want to spend on audio, it may be wiser to avoid the computer speaker market entirely and look into piecing together a set of higher-end parts. The computer speaker market tends to start pumping up wattage without making any quality improvement - you can usually get more volume, that's all. If you are buying a speaker system designed for PCs, research the systems beforehand so you can be certain of getting one that promises clarity rather than just simple wattage. (Note: speaker power is usually measured in RMS Watts. However, some cheap speakers use a different measure, PMPO which appears much higher.)

Headphones can offer good sound much more cheaply than speakers, so if you are on a limited budget but want maximum quality they should be considered first. There are even headphones which promise surround-sound, though opinions on this are usually not good.

Building the physical computer

Now that you have selected your parts, you get to what is arguably the more fun part of the process, and that is actually building the computer.

Preparation

Find a dry, well-ventilated place to do your work. You should have plenty of light to see your components with, and if possible, you should choose an area without carpet on the floor, as carpet tends to attract a lot of static, and most of this can be averted by choosing a non-conductive floor surface such as floorboards, or tiles. Make sure you don't do this in an unfinished basement!

To assemble your components, you will need a basic toolkit. For this kit, you will need a phillips-head (cross-shaped) screwdriver, and an anti-static wrist strap, for grounding yourself with (these can be purchased at your local electronic supply store) - this can often be a huge saving over the amount of money that you waste by destroying your components with static electricity. Do not be tempted to connect yourself directly to a tap or other grounded object with only a length of copper wire, if the machine is still plugged in and there is an electrical fault, the consequences could be fatal. Anti-static wrist straps have a high resistance, thus limiting any potential current flowing through your body to safe levels.

Unpack all the components, and put them on top of the anti-static bags they came in, as this will prevent stray static from reaching your components. Make sure you read the following section, as it contains some important safety information.

Safety Precautions

1. Dismantling electronic components such as your Power Supply or Monitor is an extremely dangerous thing to do - do not do it! They contain several high-voltage exposed components, and can cause you severe electric shock if you touch them. So, please, don't even think of trying.

2. Nobody except you is at fault if you shock your components with static electricity. Make sure that you take the precautions in the previous paragraph to ground yourself from static electricity, such as with an anti-static wrist strap or grounding mat. (Note: if you really must work on a computer and haven't got proper anti-static equipment, it is *usually* OK if you make sure that you don't move about much; are not wearing any static-prone clothing; handle components by the edges; and regularly (once a minute or so), touch a grounded object.)

3. Please construct your computer in a dust free enviroment! The worst thing for components (besides static and it mostly affects fans) is being clogged with dust. If this occours, the fans will fail, and cause your system to overheat and fail. However, if they are clogged, just buy a can of compressed air and blast the fans with it to clean them.

Construction

Motherboard and Power Supply

Start by putting your case down on your work surface, with the side opposite of the case door facing down, and open the case. Many cases include power supplies that are already installed on the back of the computer. However, if you buy a power supply separately, install the PSU in the top at the back of the case. Then try to find the motherboard standoffs that should have come with the case. They are screws with screw holes on the top.

Insert the standoffs into the holes on the motherboard plate in the case that correspond with the holes on your motherboard and screw them into the bottom of the case. Also remove the I/O Shield that came with the case, and put in the I/O Shield that came with your motherboard. Insert the motherboard by placing it into the open case. The ports in the upper left hand corner should line up with the I/O Shield and go through the holes in it. The screw holes should line up with the motherboard standoffs. Put a screw into each hole in the motherboard with a hole below it.

Now that you have your motherboard in, you may plug in the other components.

CPU

An example of a CPU socket, Socket A

As installation of the different makes of CPU can differ between brands, it is generally safer to refer to the manufacturer's instructions, that are provided with the CPU. If you are using a thermal paste with your CPU, follow the directions that came with them for details on how to apply it.

The **two things that go wrong the most often** and most expensively (minimum of a killed CPU, sometimes more) in building one's own computer are both related to the CPU and its cooler:

1. Switching the computer on "just to see if it works" before adding any CPU cooling unit. Without cooling, CPUs heat up at extreme rates (a CPU heats up anywhere between ten times and a thousand times as fast as a cooking area on your stove!) By the time you will get the first display on the screen, your CPU will already be severely overheating and might be damaged beyond repair.

2. Mounting the CPU cooler improperly. Read the instructions that came with your CPU and cooler very carefully and ensure you are using all components in the correct order and correct place.

Make sure you get a cooler that is compatible with the CPU you have. Most brands come with multiple mouting brackets that will suit all different chipsets, but it's best to check for compatibility just in case.

If using thermal paste, apply it only to the CPU die (the square piece of silicon in the middle of the CPU) and do so sparingly -- most modern CPUs take no more than a grain of rice sized dab of thermal paste. Some people do like to wipe some onto the heatsink's surface and then wipe it smoothly off so that bits of it may get into tiny holes for better heat transfer. If using a thermal pad supplied with your cooler, make sure you remove any protective tape just before installing and do not get it dirty - and do not combine thermal pads with thermal paste, it's either one or the other. Then, check that you install the cooler in the right orientation and that you set it flat on the CPU die without exerting undue pressure on any edges or corners - the latter can make small pieces of the die break off, killing the CPU.

One option you may consider, before installing the heatsink, is to "lap" the heatsink, which means to smooth out the bottom surface. To do this, start by sanding in smooth circular motions with a coarse grain sandpaper to smooth out the worst of the uneveness, then, as it starts to get smoother, switch to a finer grained sandpaper (the numbers go up as the sandpaper is finer, so something such as 60 is coarse while 220 will be very fine.) If you get it right, it should have a surface which feels completely smooth to the touch where you can almost see a reflection in it. Some companies producing heatsinks lap the surface themselves and this will be unnecessary, but, it is very rare. A lapped heatsink is far more effective due to having better contact with the chip.

Tighten the cooler using only the specified holding devices - if you did everything right, they will fit. If they don't fit, check your setup - most likely something is wrong. After mounting the cooler, connect any power cables for the fan that is attached onto the cooler. Then, if everything is seated tightly and firmly, you can safely run your first test, making sure the CPU fan does run (you have a few seconds of safety margin here, but if the fan is not running, switch off the system and check your cabling quickly.)

RAM

Next, you will need to install your RAM. Start by pushing on the levers on both sides of the DIMM socket, so that they move to the sides. Do not force them too hard.

If you install a floppy disk drive, the cable is very similar to the IDE cable, but with fewer wires. Floppy drives do not have master/slave. BUT the floppy disk connector is not usually keyed, and will go in either way up! One wire in the IDE cable will be coloured differently: this is pin 1. There is usually some indication on the floppy drive as to which side this is. The power plug for a floppy is 4 pins in a line, but rather smaller than a molex one.

Expansions and Connections

Now, install any PCI cards that you have. These generally include sound cards, network cards and TV tuners. These fit into the white slots that are just below your AGP slot.

Also plug in any power cords, including the 20pin and the 4 pin cords that you haven't plugged in yet. Before you finish up and power it up, you need to connect the power/reset buttons and front panel lights. The plugs from the front of the case will be labeled. The pins on the motherboard may be labeled, but they will be difficult to read because they are small. See the foldout that came with the motherboard for where to connect these connectors. The front panel LEDs are polarised: usually the positive wire is white.

next, close the case and take your computer to where you will be using it. Plug in the power, mouse, keyboard, monitor, and any other peripherals you may have to the computer.

Power Up

Then press the power button... If black smoke appears (it shouldn't, unless your power supply or cooling systems are really bad), or if the computer doesn't do anything, check the steps above to make sure you haven't missed anything. Give special attention to the cables and power connections. If the computer does appear to come on, but, you hear beeps, listen carefully to the beeps and then turn it off and refer to your motherboard's manual for the meaning of the beeps. Some boards have an optional diagnostic device, usually a collection of LEDs, which when properly plugged in will inform you of the nature of the problem. Instructions for installing this as well as the meaning of it's display should be in the manual for the motherboard. If it turns on but the only thing that comes on is your power supply, turn off your computer. This probably means something is shorted, and leaving it on could damage the parts.

At this point, you will wish to set certain options in the Computer's BIOS (usually be pressing 'F1' or 'Del' a few seconds after boot.) These options will be explained in the motherboard manual. In general, the default options are OK, but you may wish to set the computer's hardware clock to the correct time and date. The BIOS is also where you determine the default boot order of the system, typically Floppy, then CD-ROM, then Hard Disc.

If you want a further quick test, before you install an operating system, you may find a bootable CD-ROM such as Knoppix extremely useful.

Choosing and installing the computer's software

Once you have a working computer, the major difference between purchasing an OEM computer, and building your own is that you will also need to source your own software. If you make informed decisions and select the right pieces of software you can avoid many hidden costs that are often charged to your computer, such as the so-called "Windows Tax", charged to every new OEM computer. Installing operating systems (OSes) and software to your own specifications can greatly improve performance.

This section will attempt to explore the key options that you have when setting up your computer for use.

Operating System(s)

The first thing to do after you have a working PC is install an operating system. You have the option of installing more than one, as well. The first option, and the one taken by most people, is to just install Microsoft Windows, of which the current version is Windows XP. Another option is to install a <u>Linux</u> system (an <u>Open Source</u>/<u>Free Software</u> operating system). There are many other operating systems to choose from as well, notably the <u>BSDs</u>, which are also open source operating systems. Note that you also have the option of installing more than one operating system in what is called a multiboot setup.

If you are going to install both, install Windows XP first. This is because Windows overwrites the software that Linux requires to start up, even if something's already there. If you install Windows before all of your other systems, you will be able to easily boot into all of them.

Installing Windows

The installation of Windows is relatively easy. Push the button on the front of the PC, put the CD-ROM in your optical drive, and follow the on-screen instructions. Partitioning the hard disk(s) is different if you are dual-booting or going with just XP. If you are doing a plain Windows-only install, just allocate all of the hard drive to XP.

If you are dual-booting, some extra considerations must be taken. NTFS, which is the default Filesystem that Windows uses, is not very well supported outside of Windows. Linux support is up to the point where we can read, but not write, an NTFS filesystem. However, it does have some advantages over FAT32, in that a 4GB file size limit no longer exists. Likewise, Windows has no support for any of the standard Linux Filesystems. If you are going to be switching between the two frequently, then it might be in your best interest to create a FAT32 for both operating systems to use.

When it comes the time to partition the hard disk(s), remember to leave space for Linux (if you're installing it - a good amount is somewhere in the order of a third of your total hard disk space). You may want to have a spare FAT32 partition (of around 1 third of your disk space), on which to share documents between Windows and Linux, as Linux's support for NTFS disks is good, but not perfect. You should also modify the table as necessary - you may not need as much space for Windows or you may need more in your FAT32 transfer area. But you must ensure that you leave at least 3GB for your Windows installation, since the standard installation of Windows takes up about 2 GB of hard drive space, and it is always wise to leave a bit extra on, to allow for any changes that may occur.

If you are installing Windows on a RAID drive, or a SATA drive in most cases you are going to have to provide the Windows installer drivers to access the hard drive on the raid controller. To do this while Windows install is at the blue screen, at the bottom it will read "Press F6 to install any third party SCSI or RAID drivers." Later during the install it will come up with a screen says "Setup could not determine the type of one or more mass storage devices installed in your system, or you have chosen to manually specify an adapter." At this screen you are going to want to hit 'S' to "Specify Additional Device," another screen will pop up asking you to insert the floppy disk containing the drivers, followed by a screen asking you to choose the appropriate driver out of the set contained on the disk (most disks will have a for each of the major Windows operating systems).

Installing Linux

Before installing Linux, you need to be aware there is no single version of Linux. There are many, each containing many different quirks of operation. The Linux distribution that is right for you is something only you can decide, although there are many popular ones. Some of the more frequently suggested distributions include: Mandriva Linux, Ubuntu and Fedora Core Linux - since they are generally the more user-friendly ones. Distributions that tend to be more overwhelming to new-comers are: Debian, and Slackware - but they certainly have many advantages of their own. This is by no means a complete list, and there are many other distributions that you can select from: for more help in picking a distribution see the Linux Distro Guide or Distrowatch. If you are more comfortable with computers, <u>Gentoo</u> will generally run fastest, but it is much harder to install.

Installation instructions for Linux vary greatly between the distributions, so no instructions will be given here, but look out for a section that installs software called GRUB or LILO. Upon installation, you should be prompted about whether you have other operating systems (OS) (such as Windows), make sure that all operating systems on your computer are listed (otherwise you won't be able to boot them). The install for most distributions takes up about 4 gigabytes of hard drive space, however this figure varies from distribution to distribution.

Security

After installation, your priority should be security.

A newly installed Windows XP computer can be attacked within moments of being connected to the Internet. To avoid having your new computer attacked, install a firewall, or activate the one that came with your OS. Both Windows and Linux have in-built firewalls: In some Linux distributions, it is enabled by default; in Windows XP Service Pack 2, it can be found in the program in your control panel.

As soon as you are on the internet, run your operating system's update facility to fix any security flaws that have been found since your CD was printed. To do this under Windows, simply click on your Start Menu, click on 'All Programs', and then click on

Windows Update, and follow the instructions. You can also switch on "Automatic Updates" from the Security Center program mentioned above. The method of updating your Linux Operating system varies greatly from distribution to distribution. It is perhaps easiest to update the OS from Debian-based distributions such as Debian, Ubuntu and Linspire, where you simply have to type

```
apt-get update
apt-get dist-upgrade
```

into a terminal window, and if your computer will be switched on overnight, it is very easy to set these programs to run automatically in the background.

Programs such as Anti-Virus, Anti-Spam and Anti-Spyware of commercial quality or better can be found quite easily: Windows programs are listed in the software section below.

An important point to note is that security software is one of the more important things to be set up rather than other applications first. In one case, a freshly-assembled computer running Windows XP with no security precautions taken was hit by the Blaster worm as soon as it was connected to the Internet, and has picked up a variety of spyware after only visiting a few websites; forcing the owner to reformat the hard disk and redo installation of the OS.

Drivers

Now that your computer is relatively secure, you will need to install <u>drivers</u> for your various pieces of hardware.

Instead of installing drivers from CDs, it is generally a better idea to download drivers from the Internet (if you have a broadband connection) because these are usually more up to date, and can be significantly faster, and can improve your computer's efficiency greatly. Even if something seems to working fine, downloading new drivers may help. Your computer may be working perfectly, but with slightly slow performance. Downloading drivers for your motherboard's chipset can often help. Finally, many monitors will not go above a certain refresh rate without its driver, which may be of great concerns to gamers.

If you are using Windows, you can generally find drivers for your selected hardware at its manufacturer's website. Most Linux computers already have all of the drivers installed, with the exception of proprietary modem and graphics drivers. If you can't find your required driver, a simple <u>Google</u> search will yield the best results.

Software

Finally, load it with some good quality software. The majority of what you need will be available for free, on both forms of operating system, including Word Processors and Anti-Virus. I generally suggest the following for each system:

Windows

- Web Browser: Mozilla Firefox or Slimbrowser
- E-mail Client: Mozilla Thunderbird
- Office Suite: OpenOffice.org
- Disc Tools: CD Burner XP
- Instant Messenger: Gaim or Trillian
- Media Player: Nullsoft Winamp or iTunes or SnackAmp
- Anti-virus: AVG Anti-Virus, Free Edition or avast!Antivirus Home edition or ClamWin
- Security: Spybot: Search & Destroy, Ad-Aware Personal Edition, K9 Anti-Spam and ZoneAlarm Free Edition
- Compression: 7-Zip,IZArc

Linux

Unlike with Windows, on a Linux system the majority of the software that you will want for your computer is already included. You will probably not need to download anything. Most Linux distributions have a package manager (Portage for Gentoo, APT for Debian-based distros like Debian and Ubuntu, etc.) For some distributions, simply download RPM files from your distribution's web site.

If they aren't already installed by your distribution, I recommend:

- Web Browser: Mozilla Firefox
- EMail Client: Mozilla Thunderbird
- Office Suite: OpenOffice.org
- Instant Messenger: Gaim
- Media Players: Rhythmbox, amaroK (depending on what desktop environment you use) or Beep Media Player
- Movie/DVD Player: Xine or MPlayer
- Desktop Environment: KDE or GNOME
- Windows Compatibility Layer: Wine
- x86 Emulator/Virutalizer: QEMU
- PPC Emulator: PearPC

Additional Software

For additional software some exelent sources of free and open-souce software are

- <u>Tucows</u> a downloads site with freeware, shareware, open-source as well as commercial software. It has many mirrors all over the world for speedy downloads from local servers.

- <u>SourceForge</u> a site featuring many OpenSource projects. You can start your own, or get software for almost every need. Most projects have Linux and Windows versions. The mirror system isn't as large as Tucows, but you can still usually get a mirror on the same continent.

Overclocking

Overclocking (OC) is taking your computer components above their recommended speed settings.

"Overclocking is the practice of making a component run at a higher clock speed than the manufacturer's specification. The idea is to increase performance for free or to exceed current performance limits, but this may come at the cost of stability."

Think of the 3GHz on your new 3GHz Pentium 4 as a speed limit asking to be broken. This can be done to several components in your computer. This often takes advantage of the fact that many manufacturers mark higher end components as lower in order to meet demand for a lower end component. You will be able to get extra performance out of your components for free. It is possible to get performance that is not possible even when using the top of the line components. And you can buy cheaper parts, and then OC them to the clock speed of the higher end component.

WARNING: OVERCLOCKING WILL VOID THE WARRANTY ON THE PARTS BEING OVERCLOCKED. DOING SO MAY ALSO CAUSE SYSTEM INSTABILITY, AND MAY ALSO CAUSE DAMAGE TO COMPONENTS AND DATA. BE CAREFUL AND CAUTIOUS WHEN OVERCLOCKING.

Things that can't be overclocked

Although it is possible to overclock many of the components of a computer (such as the CPU, FSB frequency and video card), it is not possible to overclock many components. For example, it is not possible to increase the read/write speed or access time of a hard disk or CD-ROM drive. The only solution to improving the performance of these components is to use faster components in the first place. Many OEM computers have the CPU frequency locked. (But you wouldn't be reading this guide if you're using an OEM computer, would you?)

Components

CPU

The CPU's clock speed is the FSB clock speed (base, not effective speed) times the CPU's multiplier. On most newer CPUs, the multiplier is locked, so you will have to adjust the FSB clock speed (However, it might be possible to 'unlock' the chip's multiplier on some older chips. See CPU Locking.) The FSB is not adjustable on a few motherboards, and many OEM systems. The FSB and multiplier, if not locked, are adjustable from within the BIOS. Note that upping the FSB clock speed also increases the clock speed of many other components, including RAM. When increasing the FSB clock speed, only do so in small increments of a few MHz at a time. After you do this, boot up your computer to make sure it works. If your computer successfully boots, increase the FSB some more. If it won't boot, lower the FSB until your computer properly boots up. Repeat until you have the highest setting with which your computer will boot up. Next test your OC to make sure it is stable with a burn application, or any application that uses 100% CPU power. If a crash or reboot results, lower the FSB speed some more until it runs smoothly. On some motherboards you are also able to change the voltage of the CPU and other components in order to help stabilize the system. However, this increases the components' heat output and can harm or shorten the life of your system.

Video Card

Two different parts of a video card may be overclocked, the GPU (Graphics Processing Unit) and the RAM. In addition, disabled pipelines on a video card may also be enabled through third-party drivers, third-party software, or direct hardware modifications depending on your video card type. Overclocking a video card is usually done through third-party or proprietary software.

Recent ATI proprietary Catalyst drivers feature an interface called Overdrive that allows for dynamic GPU frequency scaling based on its temperature and load. Increase the load, the clock rate increases for performance, but it's balanced against the increasing temperature. Sufficient for simple increases in overall performance, but doesn't allow for the best performance increase which requires overclocking the memory. For this you need third-party applications or drivers. An example is ATITool. This program has many options, including GPU and memory overclocking, temperature monitoring, and fan control allowing for a much more complete solution to overclocking ATI based video cards. As for example drivers, for ATI there are many, omegadrivers.net is one of them, also hosted there are nVidia drivers as well. Both of which include integrated overclocking and many unlocked features, even including enhanced image quality for nVidia-based cards. nVidia video cards can also be

OCed through a hidden feature in the driver called coolbits.

The most important thing to remember about overclocking a video card is cooling. This can't be stressed enough. Just the same as a CPU can be damaged or have a shortened lifespan by overclocking or excessive and prolonged heat, so can a video card. In the past year many inexpensive and easy to install options have surfaced for cooling a video card, from adhesive ram heatsinks to attach to un-cooled ram chips, to rather expensive water-cooling solutions. A good midpoint (both in cost and effectiveness) solution is to purchase and install a direct exhaust, "sandwich" cooling solution. Direct exhaust means all air from the cooling fan is blown across the video card and directly out of the computer case, usually using the open PCI slot below the AGP (or PCIx) slot. This allows for substantially lower GPU temperatures. A sandwich cooler is two aluminum or copper heatsinks, shape formed for a particular video card, that "sandwiches" the video card in between the two and are usually connected by some kind of copper heat pipe which allows for the hotter side to convey heat to the cooler side for dissipation. The GPU should never surpass 60 degrees celsius for optimal performance and to avoid damaging the card. Most of the latest video cards are rated to go up to 90c, but this is NOT recommended by anyone. The optimal temperature for a video card is 40-55c for the card itself (the GPU's temperature differs depending on which you have,) but the lower you can get it, the better.

One important thing to note. Many think that the option which says "AGP voltage" in their BIOS can be used to "voltmod" a video card to get a bit more power out of it. In fact, it's used for something else, and raising the AGP voltage can and probably will cause damage to a video card.

Getting the few extra MHz out of a chip

Cooling

When increasing the speed of any computer components you are making the components work harder and by doing so they output more heat. Heat can cause system instability so cooling is necessary to help keep your components stable at higher speeds. Without good cooling you could harm or shorten the life of your system. CPU temperature can usually be checked from within the BIOS. However, these are inaccurate as your CPU is under almost no load in the bios. SiSoftware Sandra may be used within Windows to check temperature. This should be done when your CPU has been under a heavy load for a while for optimum results. There are three types of cooling that are generally accepted for overclocking: Air, water, and peltier.

With both air cooling and water cooling some type of transfer material is needed to move the energy away from the sensitive electronics. The deviced used for this purpose is a heatsink. The two most popular heatsink materials are Aluminium and Copper. The heatsink that is stock on factory computers by major manufacturers (Dell, Gateway, IBM) is usually made of aluminium, which has satisfactory heat transfer characteristics. However when overclocking more heat is being produced from the increase in power consumption and in order to obtain lower tempertures a material with better heat transfer properties is important. For this reason Copper is the material that offers the best ratio of price/performance.

Power

Chips at higher speeds may need more power. Raising the vcore voltage on a CPU might enable it to go at slightly faster speeds but by doing so you add more heat output from the CPU. The vcore of a processor is the voltage at which a chip is set to run at with the stock speed. This voltage may need to be changed when the multiplier is raised because the chip will be drawing more power. If there is not enough power then the chip will begin to make mistakes and give bad data results. Good cooling is needed to keep the system stable at higher speeds. Raising the vcore too much may harm or shorten the life of your system

Note: increasing the speed (multiplier or fsb) without changing the voltage will not increase heat output. Heat is generated when more voltage (energy) is supplied to the cpu. Having said that, increasing the multiplier or fsb without adjusting the voltage may make your system unstable (undervolt).

Silencing

In contrast to overclocking, you may prefer to silence your computer. Some high-performance PCs are very loud indeed, and it is possible to reduce the noise dramatically. Note that quieter computers sometimes run slightly hotter, so you need to monitor carefully what you do. Usually you can't overclock and silence at the same time. Main sources of noise are: Fans (CPU, case, power supply, motherboard, Graphics card), and Hard disks. One should be able to sit next to the computer, and hear birdsong from outside!

Fans

The noisiest part is usually the CPU fan: the Intel-supplied fan-heatsinks are particuarly loud, although they do provide good cooling. Some BIOSs allow you to slow the CPU fan down automatically when it is not too hot - if this option is available, turn it on. Also, you can get 3rd party coolers, which are designed to be less noisy: for example, those made by Zalman. Noisy power-supplies simply have to be replaced with quieter ones. The case fans can be slowed down by using fan-speed controllers, or resistors (but beware of ensuring sufficient cooling). Motherboard and lower-end graphics-card fans can usually be replaced with a small passive heatsink. Large diameter (120 mm), high quality fans are much quieter than small diameter ones.

Hard disk

The hard disk can also be rather noisy, with both clicks and whirring. A good solution is to mount it on rubber mounts. But do ensure good cooling of the hard drive: running a hard drive moderately hot can reduce its lifespan to under a year! Some mounts are designed to provide both extra cooling and silencing, such as the heat-pipe coolers. Spinning the HDD down when not in use will also reduce noise, but it can reduce the life of the drive.

For some harddisks, at present from <u>Maxtor</u> a software tool exists, which can adjust noise/performance ratio to what you need. The technique is called *acoustic management*. This, of course, needs drive that supports it.

Completly silent computers will need to use solid state memory like flash ram or eeprom. This is more expensive and has less capacity than a hard drive, but completly silent.

Other

- Quiet cases are available, containing noise-damping accoustic foam.

- Underclocking will reduce system performance, but you can also then reduce the CPU voltage, and power consumption. The converse of the diminishing-returns law for overclocking is that underclocking can prove surprisingly effective.

- The really obvious, but surprisingly effective: keep the computer under your desk, rather than under your monitor.

Congratulations! If you've got this far through the book, you must have done something right. You now have a computer built entirely to your own specifications, budget, and personality. You've learnt more than is possible to learn from reading any PC Hardware book.

You have a new computer. Great. But it won't always be new. Here are some tips to keep it looking as shiny as ever:

First, always try to look for good deals. If you see a computer part for a good price, think about it, because it is always easier to spread the cost of upgrading a computer over a long time. Although, there is no reason to go overboard and always be on the cutting edge (unless you like playing high-end computer games such as Doom 3 or Half-Life 2).

Second, remember to keep updating your software. Log on to the internet regularly and update:

1) Your Virus Checker. This is important. An unprotected computer is not good. Loss of data, random hardware crashes and incredibly annoying glitches can all be the result of viruses.

2) Your Operating System(s). Update your operating system regularly to download patches for holes which viruses may enter your computer by, new features, and other cool stuff. These two tasks can be scheduled to run in the middle of the night. Just remember to leave your internet connection on.

Third, occasionally (every two or three months is plenty) unplug your computer from the wall, take off the side panel, and blow out the dust with a can of compressed air, making sure to clean out the power supply as well. Be sure to not just relocate the dust from one part of the system to another but to actually blow it out. Doing this will improve the airflow inside your PC, lower the temperature, and thus give the computer a longer life. Not doing this can cause some components (such as power supplies) to eventually break a lot sooner than you were prepared for.

We have Book Recommendations for you

Automatic Wealth: The Secrets of the Millionaire Mind--
Including: Acres of Diamonds, As a Man Thinketh, I Dare
you!, The Science of Getting Rich, The Way to Wealth, and
Think and Grow Rich [UNABRIDGED]
by Napoleon Hill, et al (CD-ROM)

Think and Grow Rich [MP3 AUDIO] [UNABRIDGED]
by Napoleon Hill, Jason McCoy (Narrator) (Audio CD)

As a Man Thinketh [UNABRIDGED]
by James Allen, Jason McCoy (Narrator) (Audio CD)

Your Invisible Power: How to Attain Your Desires by Letting
Your Subconscious Mind Work for You [MP3 AUDIO]
[UNABRIDGED] by Genevieve Behrend, Jason McCoy (Narrator)
(Audio CD)

Thought Vibration or the Law of Attraction in the Thought
World [MP3 AUDIO] [UNABRIDGED]
by William Walker Atkinson, Jason McCoy (Narrator)
(Audio CD)

Thought Vibration or the Law of Attraction in the Thought
World & Your Invisible Power (Paperback)

The Law of Success, Volume I:
The Principles of Self-Mastery (Law of Success, Vol 1)
by Napoleon Hill (Paperback - Jun 20, 2006)

The Law of Success, Volume II & III:
A Definite Chief Aim & Self Confidence
by Napoleon Hill (Paperback - Aug 15, 2006)

Get Published!

BN Publishing helped authors publish more titles. So whether you're writing a romance novel, historical fiction, mystery, action and suspense, poetry, children's or any other genre, we can help you reach your publishing goals.

Paperback

Reach 20,000 retail accounts in the U.S. (including chains, independents, specialty stories, and libraries).

Including:

www.amazon.com

www.amazon.co.uk

www.amazon.ca

www.bn.com

www.powells.com

www.ebay.com

and more...

Your book will be included in a physical catalog that will go out to over 20,000 retail stores.

When your title is entered into our library it will automatically appear in the bookstore and library databases.

Our United States and United Kingdom based sales teams works with publisher clients based throughout the world who want to print books in the United States and United Kingdom, or reach the North American, UK and wider European markets through our broad distribution channel partners.

If we decide to publish it:

we will send you 2 free copies of the finished book;

we will give you 10% royalty of the selling price of each book copy sold (selling price = the price the book is sold by BN Publishing to wholesalers or other resellers);

 and if you wish to have more copies of your book, we will sell you the book for two thirds of the list price.

Please send us more information about your book to info@bnpublishing.com

BN Publishing

Improving People's Life

www.bnpublishing.com

BN Publishing

Improving People's Life

www.bnpublishing.com

BN Publishing

Improving People's Life

www.bnpublishing.com

BN Publishing

Improving People's Life

www.bnpublishing.com

BN Publishing

Improving People's Life

www.bnpublishing.com

www.ingramcontent.com/pod-product-compliance
Lightning Source LLC
La Vergne TN
LVHW042341060326
832902LV00006B/311